How to Write an Effective College Application Essay

How to Write an Effective College Application Essay

The Inside Scoop for Students

Kim Lifton and Susan Knoppow

Wow Writing Workshop

Published by Wow Writing Workshop, LLC
Copyright 2017 Kim Lifton & Susan Knoppow
ISBN

ISBN: Library of Congress Control Number:
ISBN-13: 9781973918356

ISBN-10: 1973918358

Second in a series by Kim Lifton and Susan Knoppow

**FIRST: HOW TO WRITE AN EFFECTIVE COLLEGE
APPLICATION ESSAY, THE INSIDE SCOOP FOR PARENTS**

Table of Contents

Introduction

Many students just like you have come to us asking for help understanding college application essays. They want to get it right, but they're not sure how. We're glad you found us. We are national experts on writing and application essays, and we have answers for you. We wrote this guide to share insight and provide tips so you can respond to any college application essay question.

At its core, the college essay is all about reflection. In this book, we'll clarify the mixed messages that confuse students, and help you make some sense out of the noise. The task doesn't have to be so daunting.

When you are done reading this guide, you will know:

- What the college essay really is, and how to write one (or ten) with minimal stress.
- How to read and break apart an essay prompt so you can understand it.

- How to respond to the prompt with an essay that admissions officers will want to read.
- How to reflect on who you are and what you want readers to know about you that might not be apparent from the rest of your application.
- What to ask reviewers to look for when they read your essay.

Wow has been teaching students how to write college application essays and grad school personal statements for years. We are professional writers and teachers who know the college admissions industry inside and out, and we understand the audience you are writing for. We speak at industry conferences, and we talk to admissions officers all the time.

We train school counselors, English teachers and independent educational consultants who want to improve their essay-coaching skills. We also work with business and nonprofit professionals, managing their biggest writing challenges, teaching them how to write, or taking on their projects ourselves. In all we do, we use the same step-by-step techniques that encourage reflection and take the fear out of writing.

In the college admissions industry, you will come across countless people who can tell you what colleges want in an essay. Most will not (or cannot) show you how to write those essays. Writing is a process, just like science or math. That's why we guide our students through a series of simple, manageable steps with clear instructions that are easy to follow.

You'll find outlines and templates for what the finished product should look like, or books full of sample essays, and videos with limited instructions. Some will tell you to follow a template based on what type of experience or story you want to share. Gimmicks and shortcuts won't help because they don't work. At Wow, we teach an approach, not a cookie-cutter template.

There's more than one way to write an application essay. It really doesn't matter if you record a story into a microphone or a video camera, or scribble ideas with a pen on a legal pad.

We'll show you how to write for college admissions officers without a pre-designed structure, without reading sample essays and without added stress. We've been working with students for a long time, and we've learned from our experience — and from our students' successes.

Year after year, Wow students get into their top choice schools. You should too. We hope *How to Write an Effective College Application Essay – The Inside Scoop for Students* puts you on the path to getting the results you want.

One

WHAT IS A COLLEGE ESSAY, ANYWAY?

As admission to the nation's most selective schools becomes increasingly competitive, the college essay has been rising in significance as well. There's a lot of information on the web and in books, and many well-meaning adults are out there trying to help you.

Unfortunately, much of the information is confusing, gimmicky or simply inaccurate. And most of it focuses on what the finished product should look like, not how to write it. We know that's not helpful.

Let's start by defining the term college essay. Simply put, it refers to any piece of writing that a college requires as part of the admissions process. You might hear about personal statements, personal insight questions, supplemental essays or short answer questions. All of them refer to this type of writing. In Chapter 2, we will explore the different types of essays and prompts. For now, we are talking primarily about personal statements, which most students will have to write for at least one application. The majority of schools do not conduct interviews, so college essays become the only opportunity to share your unique voice.

Colleges use these essays to help select a diverse class from among the hundreds or thousands of applicants whose grades, test scores and extracurricular activities can make all of you look alike. Some schools also use essays for scholarship selection. The number of essays and their length vary, depending on the colleges you apply to.

Essays are generally fairly short, ranging from 50 words for a short answer question to 650 words for a personal statement. Read the instructions closely for word or character count.

Some schools ask for just one personal statement. The University of California, on the other hand, asks students to answer four personal insight questions; each response can be up to 350 words.

There are several application platforms on the market to help streamline the admissions process. The most widespread and familiar is the Common Application. We'll tell you more about these platforms in Chapter 3.

Whenever we ask, admissions professionals at top universities across the country tell us exactly what they are looking for in a personal statement. One thing is certain: The personal statement provides an opportunity to show people who may never meet you just what kind of person you are.

When he reads a good essay, Calvin Wise, the Director of Recruitment for Johns Hopkins University, gets excited and will share it with colleagues. He doesn't see any reason to share grades and test scores. Just like admissions officers at other highly selective schools, Wise expects 4.0 GPAs and top scores on the ACT, SAT and AP exams.

"We need to dig deeper," Wise reminds students. "That's where the essay comes into play. That's where we find out more about the student. We are looking for your story. Academically, we are glad you've done well. We want to know who you are. What did your experience mean to you? How did it shape you?"

Colleges use the essays in different ways. There is no rubric for a good essay, but the ones that stand out all share a few common features. Regardless of the prompt, they:

- Answer the question.
- Showcase a positive trait or characteristic.
- Sound like a high school student.
- Illustrate something meaningful about the student.
- Demonstrate reflection.

The key word here is reflection. The essay should always show insight into who you are. Does the experience you write about have to be earth shattering? No. Does it have to illustrate an "aha" moment? Not at all. It is a reflection on something that has meaning to you. It doesn't matter what that is. There's no magic answer. No secret sauce. Not even a shortcut. The essay is one (very important) piece of a holistic admission process.

Shawn Felton, the Director of Undergraduate Admissions at Cornell University, reviews thousands of applications each admissions cycle. That's a lot of entrance essays. What delights him? A story that rounds out an applicant's package, and an essay that helps him understand who the person is.

"We want to put a face to the pile of paper," Felton explains. "It is part of a number of identifiers that deliver who you are as a person."

What turns him off? Stories that are not genuine, do not answer the prompt, or fail to give him any insight into the applicant's character. He does not like it when students try too hard to impress him, or write essays that seem forced or inauthentic.

"The essay is not something to be cracked," he cautions.

Here's the simplest reason you need to put the same effort into every essay required by a school: They can make a difference in helping colleges decide whom to admit. At a moderately selective school (60% admit rate and higher), where more applicants hear yes than no, students who meet certain academic requirements generally get admitted. For students who don't quite meet the standards but are not so far off, the essay can push a student into the admit pool.

At a selective school (40% admit rate and lower), where more applicants hear no than yes, the essay is even more important. It is used to distinguish one student from the others. A personal narrative helps round out the application.

In any case, there are a lot of moving parts in this process, and nothing is guaranteed. You might never know how many applicants have the same GPA and test score as you in any given year, or how you measure up in other ways.

The best advice we can offer you is to put your best effort into every essay. The essay is an opportunity to make yourself more three-dimensional in the eyes of someone you may never meet.

According to a survey by the National Association for College Admissions Counseling, grades and academic rigor are the most influential factors in an admissions decision. Next are test scores, followed by essays. As Felton says, it is just one of multiple selection factors in today's holistic approach to college admissions. Essays won't get a student who is not qualified into any college. However, they can help a qualified applicant get a better shot at admission to that dream school.

Colleges want some insight into your character. What did you do? What did you learn about yourself? Why does it matter? A girl who went on a volunteer trip to Central America to teach students to read learned more about herself on that trip when she jumped off a 30-foot cliff into the ocean. She wrote a riveting piece about feeling brave to overcome her fear of heights. That experience would have been relevant if it took place down the street or around the world. It wasn't impressive because it happened in Belize. It was impressive because it demonstrated reflection and growth.

Another student wrote a beautiful personal statement about finding strength when he asked a friend for support while his father was dying, even though the illness had been a family secret. This essay demonstrated that the young man could move beyond the family's fear of sharing his father's illness. It showed that he could ask friends for support. That ability to reach out made it clear he was prepared to succeed on his own on a college campus.

The best essays are simple and personal. Admissions officers tell us they like all types of stories, as long as they are genuine, show reflection and answer the prompt. While small, focused stories get their attention more than anything else, colleges are often less critical of student essays than you or your worried parents might assume.

Many of the best stories we've read focus on mundane moments when a student shows insight. Admissions professionals from Vanderbilt, Santa Clara and Rice universities shared some additional perspective with us.

- Jan Deike, Assistant Director of Admissions, Vanderbilt University: "Life is truly lived in the smaller moments, and that can make a powerful essay. But sometimes students feel that because they haven't found the cure for cancer, they have nothing to share."
- Lorenzo Gamboa, Senior Associate Director of Undergraduate Admission for Santa Clara University: The best personal statements focus on "one place, one time, one moment."
- Tamara Siler, Senior Associate Director of Admission, Rice University: "Focus on a moment you feel has defined you as a person, and as a student."

As we were writing this guide, the University of California system had just overhauled the writing requirement for admission to its nine undergraduate schools for the first time in a decade. UC officials felt the old questions were too broad. A top admissions representative for the UC system told us many of the essays they received failed to provide the university with enough information to enhance the application in any meaningful way. They made the change to generate more insightful responses to the prompts.

Associate Vice Chancellor of Admissions & Enrollment (Interim), & Director of Admissions Amy Jarich explains, she just wants to know what you care about: "What would you tell me in an elevator? Let me know that you're active and alive in the world you live in."

If you look at the University of California website, you'll see the system now refers to the prompts as personal insight questions rather than personal statements: "The personal insight questions are about getting to know you better — your life experience, interests, ambitions and inspirations. Think of it as your interview with the admissions office. Be open. Be reflective."

What UC reveals in its essay overhaul is significant in the world of college admissions. Most schools do not clearly explain that they all want the same thing as UC: reflection and insight. For a 17-year-old college applicant, that may not be so easy to do.

We know it can be hard to write about yourself, especially when the stakes seem so high. But handled properly, college essays can make or break an application. As a bonus, writing them can leave you feeling empowered, confident in your abilities and certain of your words.

It is likely you will be asked to write some type of personal statement during the journey to college; they will be read. Colleges would not ask students to write application essays if they did not read them, or use them to make important decisions about your future.

Your accomplishments will be evident from the rest of the application, which provides plenty of space for activities, scores and grades. The essay, on the other hand, offers an opportunity to broaden a college's understanding of who you are, not what you have done.

We tell our students the college essay is more of a thinking task than a writing task. They start the process by thinking about why they are writing college essays, and what they want readers to learn about them. Our students draft their essays after they are clear about their reasons for writing each story.

This can be challenging because it has nothing to do with how well you or any student performs in English class. In general, high schoolers come to the admissions process with little or no experience with this type of writing. While English teachers know how to recognize excellent writing, they look for something different from admissions counselors. Most (not all) do not know how to teach personal statement writing for the college audience.

We work with students every year who have received A's on the personal statements they wrote in AP English class; they think the essays are ready to include with their college applications. With few exceptions, we send them back to the drawing board. The essays may be beautifully written, but they usually miss the point and lack real reflection.

Colleges want reflection. Admissions readers are not grading essays for powerful prose and sentence structure. They want to know who you are.

Like it or not, the application essay is part of the college experience. The essay can help, and sometimes it can hurt. Jim Cotter, the Director of Undergraduate Admissions at Michigan State University, has been inside the admissions world for more than three decades. The essay, he explains, can help a student who is on the cusp get into

MSU. He adds "At a highly selective school, a poor statement can make the difference between being admitted or not."

If you want your application to stand out, make sure you write an essay that reviewers will take seriously. It won't be as hard as you might imagine, but it does require time, strategy and effort.

The writing process will be easier when you know how to reflect, dig a little deeper and be introspective. There's no need to worry; we're going to show you exactly what to do. As we move through the next few chapters, keep reflection and voice in mind. Voice is just as crucial as reflection in the personal statement.

When we use the term voice, we are referring to the essay's tone, sound and feel. The most successful essays sound like the people who wrote them.

Many students submit essays to us for review that do not sound like the teens who wrote them. Consider the story of Hillary, a delightful, smart young woman who was applying to the University of Michigan in Ann Arbor. Hillary came to us asking for input on a few essays she had written for her application package. Her mom told us up front that the essays didn't sound like Hillary.

While the prose was grammatically perfect, and the young woman had a knack for writing, her mom was right. The stories read as if Hillary were standing on top of a mountain, talking about someone down below. What was missing? Hillary's voice — her essence, her personality. She enjoyed writing, but like so many students, she was uncomfortable writing about herself.

We reviewed her essays and noticed she liked Dr. Seuss. The author clearly made an impression on Hillary. In fact, she quoted him liberally in all of her essays. One supplemental essay prompt asked students to write about a favorite book. We suggested that she choose something by Dr. Seuss.

"Can I do that?" Hillary asked. She assumed she should write about something weighty, like great literature, science or social criticism. Her mom had picked the book she had originally written about, but Hillary had no personal connection to it. It wasn't a favorite, but it felt like an appropriate choice for such an important assignment. We assured her that of course she could write about Dr. Seuss. This prompt was not a trick question. It asked about a book. Period. As long as the essay was genuine and was about her, she could write about almost anything. Hillary seemed relieved. She was excited to write about Dr. Seuss because the author inspired her.

We guided Hillary through a process that required several drafts. In the end, her story about why Dr. Seuss's *Oh! The Places You'll Go* was so meaningful to her was beautiful. Her voice shined through. No one could have written that essay the way she did. She later showed her essay to an admissions officer for the University of Michigan. He loved it. Hillary's dad, who expressed skepticism at first, was proud, too.

Many of our students and parents relate to Hillary's experience. Her essays evolved, and she became more confident as she immersed herself in the writing process. As soon as she relaxed, she didn't mind writing about herself. When she was done, Hillary's essays sounded like her: a bright, interesting 17-year-old girl.

Take a moment to think about voice. Your voice can set you apart, too.

Your story, told in your own voice and words, will show readers something genuine about you, something they can't get from test scores and grades or a long list of clubs, sports and other activities. What does your voice sound like? That is one of the first issues we address with the Wow Method, the step-by-step writing process we use with every student.

Just like a speaking voice, a person's writing voice is distinctive. That doesn't mean you can't sound sophisticated or intelligent. If you are funny, be funny. If you are serious, you can sound serious. Do you write in short, concise sentences? That's how you should write your essays. Do you like to use long, complex sentences full of vivid details? Then that style should show up in your essays too. Don't get distracted by the thesaurus. And don't expect to write like your mom, dad or favorite author. A college essay should be written in your voice and sound like you, a high school student who has something important to say.

A word about help from your parents: There is a fine line between getting help from a parent or any well-meaning adult and allowing them to write a sentence, paragraph or entire essay on your behalf. Parents may not always be able to tell when they've gone too far, but admissions officers know when a piece of writing does not sound like a high school student, and they don't like it. That's why your parents should never try to revise, write or otherwise "fix" your essay. If they do, the essay will sound like an adult who is trying to write in a teen's voice. Instead of helping you, they will be hurting you because the admissions team will know you did not write it all yourself.

"The tone of a 17-year-old student is far different from the tone of a parent," MSU's Cotter tells us all the time. "I can tell the difference."

Read a few of our favorite lines from Wow students, and you'll get the idea:

- At home, we ate beans, rice and ramen noodles for meals, and I was always hungry.
- I got my first pair of skates before I could walk.
- I jumped into an empty Dumpster and scrubbed it with a heavy-duty brush using Pine Sol and Comet cleanser.

- My body trembled as I heard the words, "If you hear the siren, you have 15 seconds to save your life."
- When I was in tenth grade, I waged a campaign to save my district's middle school French program.
- Because I am short, I managed to wiggle my way through the crowd to the front to see the list.
- I wanted to be a normal kid, just like them, not the kid with a sick dad.
- It was an overwhelming smell that reminded me of a thrift shop filled with unwashed clothing.
- I love the sound of the boat straining under the pressure of eight perfectly synchronized oars, and the copper taste in my mouth when I pull my absolute hardest.

These examples tell us something about the writer. They are written in different styles and different voices. Your voice cannot be copied; it's your signature.

Once you are confident with your voice, you will be able to focus on what you want colleges to know about you: the traits and characteristics that define you. When you are done with your final draft, your essay should illustrate those characteristics. We love essays about ordinary moments. Colleges do too. In fact, during a panel discussion we moderated at the New York Association for College Admissions Counseling's annual meeting at Wagner College, a senior admissions official from Barnard College told high school counselors she prefers reading essays that reflect on mundane moments. An effective college essay does not need to be written about something big. You do not have to rescue an infant from a house fire, get a million downloads for an app you developed, or teach an autistic boy how to swim, to impress admissions officers.

Some of the best essays we've read reflect on the most ordinary moments: two brothers on a bike ride through their neighborhood; a talented dancer choosing to drop all but a few of her dance classes; a boy and his sister stuck in traffic; a high school junior trying out for the pom-pom team at her new school; an aspiring baseball player watching his cousin take endless batting practice. Frequently, we learn enduring life lessons during everyday moments when our best selves emerge.

Does that mean a strong college essay must be written about a mundane moment? Not at all. If you know what you want readers to learn from reading the essay, your story is just an illustration of that characteristic or quality. The topic can be big or small, as long as it shows reflection and answers the question.

Students ask us all the time how to tell the difference between a good college essay and a bad one. We tell them "good" is relative. What looks good to an English teacher will not necessarily satisfy a college admissions officer. The admissions officer is not looking for a polished essay written, revised and edited for *The New Yorker*.

In its simplest form, a good personal statement will have a theme that answers these two questions:

1) What happened? and 2) Why does it matter?

Many other types of application essays can be judged by these criteria as well. While the story will naturally take center stage, readers will also know why the writer chose to share it.

Admissions officers are not going to get excited over a piece of writing that beautifully details an experience, then adds a generic sentence at the end, stating that the writer learned something significant. Nor will they enjoy a five-paragraph essay with an introduction, thesis statement, supporting paragraphs and a conclusion. For college admission, your story needs no introduction or conclusion.

You can search the Internet for the best ideas, or read samples, but it won't help. There is no best idea, shortcut or structure to imitate for the college essay. The best essays emerge from the writing and thinking process; they answer the question, show some insight and illustrate a positive trait about the applicant. A story that answers the prompt, is focused and demonstrates reflection should satisfy any admissions officer.

A few years ago, one of our students illustrated his determination with a simple story about memorizing the parts of the gastrointestinal intestinal tract to ace his anatomy final. Another girl wrote about finding her passion for nature in a community garden where she was pulling weeds. A boy with an autism spectrum disorder blew us away with a powerful story about his problem-solving skills. He forgot his cello for an orchestra concert and improvised his performance with a bass guitar. His story impressed admissions officers at his top-choice school, and the admission letter even praised the essay.

While these stories were beautiful, none was perfect. The college essay is not about perfection. Not even the most selective colleges expect brilliant prose from a teenage applicant. They know they are dealing with kids, so they often will cut applicants like you some slack. At the same time, they don't appreciate students throwing together sloppy essays the night before the deadline. They want to see some effort and a healthy respect for the rules of written English.

The essay is the perfect place to show colleges who you are. We encourage you to reflect and honor your voice so you can confidently share your stories.

As you begin the process, always keep in mind:

What you are writing: A story about you

Who you are writing for: College admissions counselors

Why you are writing it: 1) to illustrate something meaningful about yourself; 2) to demonstrate how you think; 3) to help admissions officers round out your application package; 4) to show that this college is a good fit

Your essay should be:

Specific: Don't write about your entire summer working on a construction site. Choose an important moment or other small piece of your experience, then demonstrate why that moment matters.

Clear: Speak in your own voice. Don't try to be funnier, smarter or more creative than you already are. Make sure you sound like yourself.

Direct: Say what you mean in plain language.

Unique: Even if your experience seems mundane, the fact that it happened to you makes it unique.

Two

Understanding the Prompts

Katie came home from school one day, flustered over a seemingly simple English class assignment: Write a personal statement for college. Katie was upset, and went to her dad for guidance.

He had never seen this side of his daughter. She could always manage her schoolwork on her own. Not this time. The teacher sent students home to write the essay with no instructions. Katie, not knowing where to start or what to do, was fixated on a topic — ice-skating. And why not? She was a competitive skater. It was integral to her life. Would that topic help her stand out, she asked her father?

The dad, Alan, knew a little bit about the essay. He had been doing some research on college admissions so he would be prepared to guide her. In fact, a few nights before she showed him the assignment, Alan had participated in one of our online parent chats. They're free and open to the public. We host them monthly to answer parent questions and provide tips for them to help their children. He was relieved he could offer assistance, but still a little surprised by his daughter's reaction to the assignment. Why was she so anxious, he wondered?

Katie was too far ahead of herself in the process, and her dad knew it. She was thinking about a topic before she understood the prompt. The topic, he told Katie, was not as significant as the subject. In other words, the essay needed to be about Katie (the subject of the essay), not ice-skating (the topic).

Katie was about to make one of the most common mistakes colleges see in application essays. She was prepared to write about an experience, rather than what she learned from it or what that experience demonstrated about her. Katie was so focused on finding a good topic that she paid little attention to the prompt, one her teacher selected from the Common Application: Some students have a background, identity, interest, or talent that is so meaningful they believe their application would be incomplete without it. If this sounds like you, then please share your story.

The key word here is "meaningful." Katie needed to reflect on her experience.

Fortunately, her father was able to guide her. He asked her the one question we use repeatedly with our students to help them slow down before choosing an essay topic: What do you want colleges to know about you beyond your grades, test scores and extracurricular activities?

After a 30-minute conversation with her father, Katie decided she wanted colleges to know she was compassionate. She felt confident she could demonstrate that trait in her personal statement.

Ultimately, she did find a topic through her experience on the ice. In her essay, Katie showed colleges she was compassionate in a focused story about a time she taught a young child how to skate. That experience could have happened at a library, teaching a child to read, or on a nearby sidewalk, teaching a child how to ride a bike. The setting did not matter because it showed introspection into Katie's character in a way that could help colleges get to know her better.

You can do this, too. But first, make sure you understand the prompt. To really understand a prompt, you will want to break it apart and determine both what the college is asking and why it is asking this question. We say this all the time, and college reps do, too. Still, year after year, the biggest mistake students make is not answering the question.

We know you don't want to fall into that category. That won't happen if you figure out what the prompt means before you sit down to write your first draft!

To learn how to read a prompt, look at the instructions for the personal statement on the Common Application:

The essay demonstrates your ability to write clearly and concisely on a selected topic and helps you distinguish yourself in your own voice. What do you want the readers of your application to know about you apart from courses, grades, and test scores? Choose the option that best helps you answer that question and write an essay of no more than 650 words, using the prompt to inspire and structure your response. Remember: 650 words is your limit, not your goal. Use the full range if you need it, but don't feel obligated to do so. (The application won't accept a response shorter than 250 words.)

These instructions are followed by seven prompts that a student can choose from. It does not matter which prompt you select; the key question is: What do you want colleges to know about you? This is your opportunity to shine, to offer readers some insight into who you are beyond grades, test scores and activities.

Now we're going to make it really easy for you to get an advantage inside the admissions office. Take a look at the Common App prompt Katie used for her class assignment:

Some students have a background, identity, interest, or talent that is so meaningful they believe their application would be incomplete without it. If this sounds like you, then please share your story.

Ultimately, an essay responding to this prompt is not about a student's background, identity, interest, talent or experience; it's about why that background, identity, interest or talent matters to the student.

Admissions officers read these essays to find out something they don't already know about you. They can tell from the application if you are on the lacrosse team or in the school orchestra, or if you worked as a researcher, a hospital aide or a bagger in a grocery store. What they don't know is how those experiences affected you or what you learned about yourself. They have no idea how you have changed. The essay is the place to share such insights.

You can respond to this prompt by sharing any type of story — a description of a significant conversation, a time when you realized something personally important — anything that truly and vividly demonstrates who you are. You do not need to climb a mountain or travel to another country to write a compelling story. Babysitting or making meatballs with grandma, navigating an icy highway or playing basketball with friends works, too.

The why (the learning or insight) is more important than the what (the experience). Keep asking the key question we use with our students, and make sure you have a clear answer before settling on an essay topic. Again, the question is this: What do you want colleges to know about you beyond your grades, test scores and extracurricular activities? You can break it up, or expand on it, too:

- What do I want colleges to know about me? Why?
- What did I do? Why? Why would a college be interested in this? What does it show about me that they can't find out from the rest of my application?
- What did I learn about myself?
- How does this experience show who I really am?

If you get stuck, "why?" is always a good question. We ask our students "why?" all the time. Katie responded to one of the seven Common Application prompts. For the application year 2017-18, the Common App offered six other, more specific prompt choices as well:

- The lessons we take from obstacles we encounter can be fundamental to later success. Recount a time when you faced a challenge, setback, or failure. How did it affect you, and what did you learn from the experience?
- Reflect on a time when you questioned or challenged a belief or idea. What prompted your thinking? What was the outcome?
- Describe a problem you've solved or a problem you'd like to solve. It can be an intellectual challenge, a research query, an ethical dilemma – anything that is of personal importance, no matter the scale. Explain its significance to you and what steps you took or could be taken to identify a solution.
- Discuss an accomplishment, event, or realization that sparked a period of personal growth and a new understanding of yourself or others.
- Describe a topic, idea, or concept you find so engaging that it makes you lose all track of time. Why does it captivate you? What or who do you turn to when you want to learn more?

- Share an essay on any topic of your choice. It can be one you've already written, one that responds to a different prompt, or one of your own design.

We explain in detail what each Common App prompt means in Chapter 6. Meanwhile, the University of California asks students to choose four out of eight Personal Insight Questions. Many institutions in Texas use the ApplyTexas application, with its own personal statement prompts. Scores of schools have begun accepting the new Coalition for Access, Affordability and Success application, which also offers four personal statement choices. And many state universities ask their own personal statement questions on their independent applications. While we cannot predict what the admissions process will look like in the future, all evidence indicates the essay will remain — and it will continue to grow in importance.

Here are some examples of what we tell our students when we're not sure they're being reflective enough in their personal statements:

- If you chose this story because it happened on a trip to Kenya, then it's about Kenya. If the same story would have been equally meaningful if it had taken place in your grandmother's backyard, then the story is about you.
- If the essay is meaningful only because you won the championship, then it's about the winning goal. If it would have been equally meaningful if you hadn't won, then it's about you, and what you learned or demonstrated about yourself.
- A sad story about poverty, lack of opportunity or uncommon obstacles is not enough to draw readers in. Show us how you faced these challenges and what that demonstrates about your character.

In addition to personal statements, students often need to write supplemental essays for the schools they apply to. Here are some tips for approaching a variety of supplement types. You can apply the same techniques we described for personal statements when parsing supplemental prompts.

"Why College X?" Essays

Many schools ask a variation on the question, "Why us?" This prompt can be one of the most challenging for students. The questions often look like these, from current and past years' applications:

Northwestern University

What are the unique qualities of Northwestern — and of the specific undergraduate school to which you are applying — that make you want to attend the University? In what ways do you hope to take advantage of the qualities you have identified?

Tufts

Which aspects of Tufts' curriculum or undergraduate experience prompt your application? In short, Why Tufts?

New York University

NYU's global network provides students with hundreds of academic areas of interest for students to cultivate their intellectual curiosity and to help achieve their career goals. Whether you are entirely undecided about your academic plans or you have a definitive program of study in mind, what are your own academic interests? Feel free to share any thoughts on any particular programs or how you might explore those interests at NYU on any of our campuses.

Cornell University College of Engineering

Tell us about an engineering idea you have, or about your interest in engineering. Describe how your ideas and interests may be realized by — and linked to — specific resources within the College of Engineering. Finally, explain what a Cornell Engineering education will enable you to accomplish.

Macalester College

What factors have led you to consider Macalester College? Why do you believe it may be a good match, and what do you believe you can add to the Mac community, academically and personally?

In every case, your answer needs to address three important areas:

1. The School: What attracts me to this college or program?

2. The Student: What do I want readers to know about me?

3. The Stories: How does what I know about the program mesh with what I want readers to know about me? How can I illustrate this intersection?

Many students have very little idea what a school offers academically, socially or culturally. Sometimes students choose a college because of the location or its status. This is not what admissions officers want to know. They need to know you will be comfortable in the big city, but they are more interested in their school and what the college or program offers. Do you have the chops to succeed academically? Are there any clubs and activities to support your interests? Why do these factors matter to you?

Each year, we meet many young people who insist that a school is perfect because the student bleeds the university's colors, feels at home inside the football stadium, and loves listening to stories around the Thanksgiving dinner table from Dad, Aunt Lisa and cousin Diana, all enthusiastic and accomplished alumni. Colleges want students to be comfortable for many reasons, but this type of answer is never sufficient. It does not answer the prompt.

Community Essays

Some schools want to find out how students might contribute to the campus community by learning about how they participate in their current community. The University of Michigan has asked this question for several years. It is a typical community essay prompt:

> Everyone belongs to many different communities and/or groups defined by (among other things) shared geography, religion, ethnicity, income, cuisine, interest, race, ideology, or intellectual heritage. Choose one of the communities to which you belong, and describe that community and your place within it.

Kim Bryant, U-M's Assistant Director of Admissions, reviews upward of 5,000 application packages each season. She's spent decades inside the admissions office in Ann Arbor. She's read essays about everything. She wants to be wowed. Here's Bryant's advice on answering the community essay prompt so she'll want to read it: "We have an amazing, vibrant, thriving community mixed up of students in athletics, strong academics, research, over 1,200 student clubs and organizations. We want to know what they do to stand out. What do they do in their community, church, high school, synagogue, and mosque? What are they going to do on our campus to make a difference in the world?"

Activity Essays

In general, colleges like to know more about a student than the sentence or two that students include on the activities section of an application or resume. When asked, "Which activity would you continue in college?" or "Tell us about one significant activity," students need to expand upon the activity by explaining what they like about it, what they find engaging about the activity, and why this is important to them.

As with all essay opportunities, make sure you know why you are sharing a story. If you write about tennis because you won six championships, that information is likely already in the application. If you write about how hard you worked to get along with your new doubles partner, and as a result became a better team player, that's something readers wouldn't already know.

One of our students wrote an activity essay about learning the value of hard work when he cleaned out a Dumpster as part of his job in the kitchen of the overnight camp he had attended for many years. His colorful description of the activity, along with what he learned, showed how hard he worked under the worst of circumstances. His essay revealed insight. That's why it worked.

Influential Person Essays

The prompts on college applications are not always as straightforward as they appear. Consider the "influential person" essay prompt, which might look like this: Indicate a person who has had a significant influence on you, and describe that influence.

Colleges do not want to read stories about Aunt Rose, a beloved first-grade teacher or the student's great-grandfather who invented the crinkle potato chip. Instead, you need to write about how this special person helped shape you, what you gained from the relationship, and why it matters to you now.

It is admirable if Aunt Rose saved five children from a burning house or won the Presidential Medal of Freedom. But what does that have to do with you? Were you one of the kids she saved? Are you a volunteer firefighter because of this experience? If not, let Aunt Rose apply to college on her own. She might even earn a scholarship for her heroic acts.

Issue Essays

Even if a college asks students to discuss an issue (racism, poverty, domestic violence, world hunger, gun control) that is relevant to them, admissions officers still want you to reflect on that issue. Consider the "issue essay" prompt, which might look like this: Discuss some issue of personal, local, national, or international concern and its importance to you.

Are you passionate about the environment? Do you follow politics like a veteran pundit? Are you a vegetarian or an advocate for the elderly? These are admirable issues, but unless you can explain what you have done as a result of this great concern, this essay won't shine. Why did you become a vegetarian? How has it affected your daily life? What insight have you gained while teaching Mom and Dad to cook tofu? Answers to questions like these demonstrate reflection.

Creative Essays

Students generally either love or hate creative essays. Here are three sample prompts from the University of Chicago, the leader of the creative, provocative prompt:

- Where's Waldo, really?
- What's so odd about odd numbers?
- If you could balance on a tightrope, over what landscape would you walk?

In addition to a personal statement, UChicago asks students to write several supplemental essays, including one that demonstrates their compatibility with the school. People who attend UChicago like questions like this. If you can't bear the question, UChicago is probably not a good fit.

The idea is to have some fun with this essay. "Write it any way you want," the school tells students. "We think of them as an opportunity for students to tell us about themselves, their tastes, and their ambitions. They can be approached with utter seriousness, complete fancy, or something in between."

Other schools offer creative prompts as well. These samples come from current and past application seasons.

ApplyTexas

You've got a ticket in hand — Where will you go? What will you do? What will happen when you get there?

University of Pennsylvania

You have just completed your 300-page autobiography. Please submit page 217.

Bucknell University

Pick a movie or novel where the protagonist makes a difficult choice. Do you agree or disagree with the decision he or she made?

Hampshire College

Create two questions that drive you.

Lehigh University

You've just reached your one millionth hit on your YouTube video. What is the video about?

Just like personal statements, supplemental essays offer a chance to round out your application package. Make the most of this opportunity.

Three

Competition and Confusion: An Industry Perspective

The competition to get into the nation's top colleges gets tougher every year, but that's not because students are smarter or more qualified than they were five or ten years ago.

It's a simple matter of impossible math.

Year after year, more kids apply for the same number of available spaces at the most selective schools. It is impossible for them all to get in.

So how can you get into that dream school when the odds are stacked against most applicants? Good question. We'll provide some tips for gaining an advantage in Chapter 4. But before we get there, we want to help you understand the admissions industry overall because college essays are just one aspect of a complete application.

Because it is so hard to get into the top name-brand schools (think Stanford, Harvard, UC Berkeley, MIT, Vanderbilt, Columbia, University of Chicago, to name a few), the students who are qualified for the most selective colleges look elsewhere to improve their chances. They use modern technology to apply to more schools than they might have otherwise considered.

Today, students can apply to multiple schools, whether they choose five or 15, using one of several streamlined applications that make the process almost seamless (though no less expensive). The most popular is the Common Application, which was used by nearly 700 member colleges and universities when this book was published, and grows every year. The Common App makes applying to college so easy that students frequently check boxes for schools they might normally ignore if more effort were required.

This practice helps colleges increase their applicant pool. It works well for schools because it makes them look more selective. If a school can accept only 1,200 students and 6,000 apply, the admit rate — or the percentage of students the school accepts — will be 20%. If 12,000 apply, the college will enroll the same number of first-year students, but the admit rate will plummet to 10%. On paper, it will look like this college has become more selective ("We accept only 10% of applicants.") This practice can be challenging for students like you who just want to get into a good college.

The Universal College Application, a spin-off from the Common App, is less known in the college world. But, like the Common App, it can be used to apply to multiple schools. Texas has its own application, called ApplyTexas, as do the University of California system, New York's SUNY schools and several other state networks.

The Coalition for Access, Affordability and Success went live in spring 2016. As we were writing this guidebook, the Coalition App was entering its second year, and most of the schools that signed on were also using the Common Application or their own applications.

These days, it may be hard to get in, but it's almost too easy to apply to multiple schools.

To see how ease of applying affects the admit numbers at popular colleges and universities, look at the University of Michigan, which began accepting the Common App in 2010. That year, applications jumped by 25%; U-M received a record 39,584 applications, and its admit rate dropped to 38.9% — the lowest percentage since 2005. Five years after joining the Common App (2015), applications to U-M surpassed 50,000, and the admit rate plunged to 26.3%.

Confused? Overwhelmed? Remember, all applications are used to help colleges decide which students to admit. That's why essays are so important. With more and more students applying to the same schools, you need to help readers see beyond your grades, scores and a list of activities.

You can be sure this trend will continue. As additional schools join consortiums to make the application process easier, they will become better known, and the numbers of applications will continue to rise.

Like other students, you might want to apply to multiple schools, and you can create a good list — complete with dream schools and more realistic choices. You might notice that the brand-name schools dominate the news, social media, college ranking lists and conversations among you and your friends. But if you conduct your own research, attend college fairs and talk to your school counselor, you'll be able to develop a list of choices that are appropriate for you.

The increasing competition to get in is not all bad news for students. Colleges, under pressure to be more inclusive and accessible, are beefing up recruiting and marketing efforts in urban and more diverse communities. If you keep your ears open, you'll probably hear about unfamiliar schools as your journey to college continues.

There are about 5,300 two- and four-year colleges in the U.S. according to the National Center for Education Statistics. More than

20 million students are enrolled in college — a number that has increased by nearly 5 million since 2000. It's a big business. Students need colleges, but colleges also need students. If you want to get a degree after high school, the odds are stacked in your favor.

In fact, some of the lesser-known schools — consider the unrated ones on the rankings lists that are academically strong but not marketed as heavily — generally give away the most cash in scholarships.

Useful, accurate and relevant information is your best friend. And the more you know, the less stress you will feel.

Before we tell you how to relieve that stress, let's review some more numbers — the ones that everyone talks about. Just to put the industry into some real perspective, we are going to focus on the dream: Getting into the most exclusive, super-selective university in this country. Today it's Stanford. Tomorrow it could be Harvard, Northwestern, Columbia or MIT. In any case, we are talking about big name brands.

In 2016, Stanford became the first school in the nation to drop below a 5% admit rate. Remarkably, that figure plummeted from the previous decade. At 4.69%, Stanford surpassed Harvard (5.2%) for the second year in a row. Next was Columbia at 6%, followed by Yale (6.3%), Princeton (6.5%), University of Chicago (7.6%), MIT (7.8%), Caltech (7.9%) and Brown (9%).

The rest of the Ivies came in under 14%; Northwestern, Johns Hopkins and Vanderbilt admitted about 10% of their applicants; Notre Dame accepted 18%.

The most selective public school was the University of California, Berkeley at 14.8%, followed by the University of North Carolina at Chapel Hill (25.8%) and the University of Virginia (28%). U-M (26.3% in 2015) had not yet reported its rate for 2016 when we gathered these figures.

Yes, you can get noticed — and have the best chance of getting attention inside the admissions office, where it matters most. Just be realistic, and once all the hard work is done (such as getting an A on the calculus final), you will want to focus on the essays.

No matter what changes in the industry, one thing remains constant: writing matters.

More schools are becoming test-optional, which means grades and writing are the most significant factors in admission. Some admit based on straight grades and test scores, but most land somewhere in the middle. Everything comes into play: grades, test scores, essays, activities and letters of recommendation.

The state of admissions has everyone up in arms. You may be confused because you don't know what colleges expect. Colleges are taking heat because they are too expensive, and admit rates have plunged to ridiculous levels. As a result, students worry about getting into college — and many fear they won't have any options.

We don't want you to worry. That's why we're giving you good, accurate and useful information to help you write your college essays.

We cannot state enough how important it is to remember that colleges are interested in character, as well as grades. If you share meaningful traits and characteristics in college essays, standing out should come naturally.

Do you have Ivy League ambitions? Hoping for a spot at your favorite Big 10 school? Or are you eyeing a great college right in your backyard? A meaningful college essay, written in your words and your voice, really can help you stand out from the crowd of other qualified students at your dream school.

We have interviewed dozens of admissions officers from major universities and small colleges alike, and they all say the same thing. Without exception, they advise students and parents to relax, take a deep breath and focus on the things you can control.

If you take the ACT or SAT four times, and that score doesn't rise accordingly, you may not be able to do anything about it. But you can improve your grades and take classes that are both challenging and appropriate. You can also write a stellar story about yourself in your application essay.

A couple of years ago, a friend took his son, a talented member of his school's rowing team, on a tour of elite East Coast colleges and universities. We asked him to let us know what he heard at those schools regarding admissions essays.

Most college representatives mentioned the essay during their presentations, but MIT took the message a step further. While talking about the quest for the perfect ACT or SAT score, the admissions representative reminded parents and prospective students that test scores merely indicate whether a student is academically ready for freshman courses.

Above a certain level, scores didn't seem to make much of a difference. In fact, the MIT rep said students trying to achieve perfect test scores were wasting their time. Instead, she suggested students put that time and effort into their essays.

Despite what you might have heard, the most selective schools do not expect application essays to be written much differently from those submitted to less selective colleges. In fact, during a college essay panel discussion, senior admissions staff members from Columbia University and Barnard College said they do not expect better quality writing from applicants to their schools. They look for reflection and an answer to the prompt. No bigger words. No better writing. Columbia and Barnard want to know how you think.

Both reps said the essay was their favorite part of the application package. The task and expectations are the same for just about every college that requires essays.

There is so much information coming from outside sources that it can be difficult for otherwise clear-headed people to differentiate between good and bad advice. As a result, colleges say they are not getting what they want, and are uninspired by many of the essays that come across their desks.

If it has not happened yet, you might soon be inundated with information promising success on the essay through gimmicks like these:

- Write it like a movie trailer or a screenplay.
- Start with a hook, or a killer opening sentence.
- Tell your story out loud, and record it.
- Buy a book of essays that worked, and model yours on one of them.
- Send us your information, and we will outline the essay and write it with you.

This is all noise. Clutter. Confusion. Instead of offering gimmicks and shortcuts, we help our students write essays that get noticed by teaching them how to reflect and share something meaningful. Sure, you can tell your story out loud into a camera, but you can also write it down on paper, type on a computer or tap the essay into a phone. Most importantly, you must tell it yourself — not "together" with a company that offers to write it on your behalf. And don't be swayed by "essays that worked" for any school. No one can imitate a sample essay and still sound authentic.

The college prep industry is rife with junk that will litter your inbox and guarantee nothing. Be careful. Why? Because it matters. This might be the first time in your life that something you write can influence your future. The task can seem daunting.

Like so many industries, the college admissions community has its own set of buzzwords. These are words you know, but in the context of applying to college and writing essays, they can be confusing.

What school representatives mean when they speak to you during college visits, college fairs and at your school is often quite different from what you hear. Admissions officers throw out words like passion, voice, leadership, grit, initiative and authenticity. To you and your friends, passion might sound like something that will drive you to greatness, like building an orphanage in a third-world country or finding a cure for cancer. You might also assume that taking initiative means starting a business or making a cool million before graduation.

Think about the word leadership. What does it mean to you? Does it sound like something that demonstrates potential to become the leader of the free world, or running for student government president, winning, and then making huge changes in the school? What about the word voice? Despite what you might assume, you don't have to sound professional or like a published author in your college essay. Just write an essay that sounds like you. Only you.

When pressed, college admissions reps tell us that they don't expect huge accomplishments from young people. They just want to know who you are.

The problem is that the message from the top (admissions) is not making its way down to you, the intended audience. No one is intentionally trying to misguide you. Well-meaning adults, including high school counselors, independent educational consultants, teachers and parents, try to help. But the message is still not getting translated accurately.

It's all part of the reason colleges continue to receive essays that are either boring, don't answer the prompts, or fail to tell them anything about the student. In this case, the essay, while it may not hurt the student, does nothing to enhance the application. Students miss out on an important opportunity to let colleges learn something meaningful about them.

We help our students cut through the clutter. You can do that too by breaking down the buzzwords so you understand what the essay is, why you have to write one or several, and what admissions officers are looking for. We'll help you start translating the message by exploring the most common buzzword: Passion.

Colleges say things like this:

- Show us your passion!
- What is your passion?
- Share your passion.
- Is there something you are so passionate about that your application might be incomplete without it?

Rather than agonize about the word passion, focus on what your audience is asking. Colleges care about core beliefs. To find yours, ask yourself questions like these:

- What do I care about?
- What do I do in my free time?
- What would I do right now if I had nowhere to be and nothing I had to do?

Maybe you walk the dog every day without being asked, or you relax before final exams by drawing cartoon figures. These activities show that you take responsibility or know how to manage stress. Colleges care about that; they care about who you are.

Both UC Berkeley's Associate Vice Chancellor of Admissions & Enrollment (Interim) Amy Jarich, and Shawn Felton, the Director of Undergraduate Admissions at Cornell University, talked about the buzzwords at a National Association for College Admissions Counseling annual meeting in San Diego. They participated in a panel we moderated called "What Admission Wants in an Essay: How to Instruct Your Students."

In a room with hundreds of counselors and educational consultants from throughout the U.S., we talked about the mixed messages that permeate the industry and ways to make essays less confusing for students. One of the counselors on the panel, Ed Schoenberg, of Bellarmine College Prep in San Jose, California, shared two powerful stories about working with confused students. His stories will help you understand what colleges mean by the words leadership and initiative.

The son of a janitor at Schoenberg's school noticed that his high school classmates were leaving the cafeteria in a mess after lunch. The student organized a group of a half-dozen kids who picked up trash so the school's cleaning staff wouldn't be overburdened. He wrote a beautiful essay that demonstrated that he cared about others and knew how to motivate his peers. What more could a college ask for?

Another of Schoenberg's students came into school one day feeling discouraged because he didn't think his life showed any aspects of initiative. The boy told his counselor he had nothing to write about.

Schoenberg asked him a few probing questions. He knew the boy played violin, and that he worked in a senior-citizen home. Asked to describe what he did at the home, the boy said he played violin there, and they talked about how he felt when he played for the seniors. Because of this conversation, the boy wrote a compelling personal statement about what he learned about himself when he took initiative and played his violin for the seniors during his volunteer shift.

Schoenberg knew how to guide the conversation to help draw out his student's best traits so he could find a story to illustrate it. But even with the best of intentions, many adults contribute to the mixed messages that students internalize.

If you can mute the outside noise that confuses you, and put this industry into some perspective, you will be in a much better position to navigate the application process – and write an effective college application essay that admissions teams will want to read.

Four

Choosing a Meaningful Topic

Preparing yourself to write college essays is one of the best gifts you can give yourself during an otherwise confusing and stressful time. The sooner you begin, the better. Contrary to popular belief, writing is not the challenge here. Exploring who you are, what matters to you and how you exhibit those traits or characteristics in the world is the tough part.

It doesn't have to be so hard. When we help our students focus up front, the rest of the process moves along much more smoothly. Before you start writing, selecting a prompt or picking a topic, you need to know which defining traits and characteristics are important enough to share with colleges. That's the first step toward reflection.

Too many students get hung up on the topic of the college essay, long before they are even ready to start the application process. They look for activities that might lead to stories, and devote a lot of time talking about their experiences and their accomplishments. That's why college essays seem so difficult. Students start in the middle without even knowing they skipped the first part of the process.

Have you been thinking about what makes a great topic? Do you think you know what you are going to write about? If so, slow down. We suggest that you take two steps backward if you plan to start your college essay with a topic in mind. Instead, focus on a few traits and qualities that make you great. How would you describe yourself?

- Are you kind? Funny?
- Are you resourceful? Curious?
- Are you industrious? Patient?
- Are you compassionate?
- What are your best qualities?

Remember the girl who wanted to write about skating? Follow her lead, and put the topic aside while you focus instead on traits and characteristics.

We've already told you that college applicants don't always stand out because of grades, test scores and unusual experiences. But it is so important; we are going to repeat it. You can make your application pop by sharing a story that illustrates what you learned from any experience or detailing what the experience shows about you. How did it affect you? Did you change? How? Again, what happened to you is important, but why it matters is critical.

It can be hard to identify your own best features. You might prefer to talk about accomplishments. Naturally, you are thinking about your future: where you will live, what job you might have, and perhaps a trip around the world. What's more, you probably have had very little or no practice writing about yourself or being reflective. That's okay.

Let's try to reflect a little. You can start now. Begin by answering these questions:

- What three words would your best friend use to describe you to a new student who came to your school?
- What do you like to do when you are not at school?
- What do your friends say about you? Are you a problem-solver? Do you like a challenge?
- I'm the kind of person who _____.
- If you were standing on a stage, and five people you never met were in the audience interviewing you for your dream job, what would you want them to know about you that they couldn't find from reading your resume?
- What makes you great?

You can answer these questions alone, or discuss them with your parents, siblings, or friends. In our experience working with students, we find that getting started is the biggest challenge. Especially because this task involves sitting still for long enough to dive deep into your mind so you can write about something personal. Let's face it, writing about yourself is hard.

Several years ago, we worked with a student named Nikki, who did not like writing about herself at all. We met her after she submitted her Common Application essay to multiple schools; she had already submitted a few supplements to three Ivies. She had two more essays to write, and she approached Wow for help.

Nikki showed us the essays she had submitted. We noticed something was missing from each story: Nikki! The essays were highly polished, but they demonstrated no connection to the writer. Anyone could have written them. Reflection was minimal. She talked about what she did, and her personal statement read like a resume. Nikki said she did not like her own writing, was not comfortable writing about herself, and allowed one of her parents to "fix" her essays. It didn't work.

She applied to some of the most selective schools in the country, and she needed something to distinguish herself from the other qualified applicants. She was just as qualified as anyone. But her essays failed to demonstrate any insight into her character.

We took Nikki through our process for the two remaining essays. She wrote beautiful and insightful pieces, including one focusing on a fateful trip to France with a French teacher. That trip and the teacher inspired her to pursue a career in international relations. While Nikki did not get into her Ivy choices, she was admitted to – and excelled in – the honors program at one of the nation's most selective public universities.

After working with Wow, she decided she liked to write in the first person. In fact, she credited Wow with teaching her how to write and she returned to us for help with personal statements when she applied to grad school for international affairs. At press time, she was about to start a master of arts program in international law and diplomacy at Tufts University's Fletcher School.

There are many ways to reflect. For the college essay, we suggest you start the process by answering the question we introduced in Chapter 2: "What do I want colleges to know about you beyond test scores, grades and extracurricular activities?"

Your answer will guide your essay.

We cannot emphasize enough that in a highly competitive admissions world in which students like you can look the same on paper, decision makers depend on personal narratives to broaden their understanding of who you are, not just what you have accomplished. Think about your best traits and characteristics, and find stories to illustrate those traits.

Your parents can help you reflect on your life so you can dig a little deeper into your own mind. Your friends can tell you what they like about you. Reach out to your siblings, too. But no one should suggest best topics. The people who know and love you can tell you what they like about you, and what they see from raising you, living with you or hanging out with you. No matter what they think they know about you, they should not tell you which trait to feature in your essay, or which story is the best example to highlight it. Just remember, colleges want to know who you are and what you want to share with them. It's all up to you. No one else. When you are able to find insight from your life experiences, you will be able to write your college essays with confidence.

As writing teachers, we know the boundaries. We know how much to help, and when to back off. We know intuitively when it is time for our students to be done. Your parents might feel pressure to do more, rather than less. The pressure comes from outside forces you and your parents may not even recognize. To be meaningful, a topic should emerge from a process of reflection. Our process takes students through that process, step by step.

When you are ready to begin your essay, remind yourself that you (the subject) are always more important in the essay than the topic, the experience or accomplishment. Your reflection on that topic is what will give meaning to the essay and help you get the attention you deserve inside the admissions office.

Five

By now, you should have a better understanding of the essay's role within the college admissions world. We've provided a snapshot of the industry, and we've explained what admissions officers expect from you. We hope to minimize the confusion, make this task less draining and provide useful information to get you through this part of the journey effectively and efficiently. This graphic illustrates our approach. We break up the process, from beginning till final draft, into three parts: content, structure and polish.

The Wow Method: Ten Steps to a Great College Essay

Step 1: Understand the Prompt
Step 2: Brainstorm Ideas
Step 3: Focus on Theme
Step 4: Free Write for Details
Step 5: Write Draft 1
Step 6: Review Prompt and Theme

> **Steps 1-6**
> **CONTENT**

Step 7: Take It from the Top
(Write Draft 2)
Step 8: Review Content and Structure

> **Steps 7-8**
> **CONTENT & STRUCTURE**

Step 9: Add the Wow Factor
(Write Draft 3)
Step 10: Edit and Proofread

> **Steps 9-10**
> **CONTENT, STRUCTURE &**
> **POLISH**

Follow the Process

The best essays emerge during the process of writing. Don't start with preconceived notions about what makes a good essay. Just write. The results might surprise you.

Content: Steps 1-6

As you begin the process, you don't need the perfect opening line, and you shouldn't worry about keeping everything in the right order just yet. In fact, you won't even start writing your first draft until step 5.

Why?

Preparation is paramount. It is critical that you understand exactly what you are trying to achieve before turning your ideas into an actual essay. By the time you finish that first draft, the content of the essay should be absolutely clear. Step 6 offers an opportunity to confirm that the content is all there.

Structure: Steps 7 and 8

Next, we concentrate on structure: making sure every part of your essay is exactly where it belongs. You will check and re-check that your essay works from every possible angle. Content is still important here. Through revision, you will likely find new and better ways to express yourself.

Polish: Steps 9 and 10

After working on structure, it is finally time to polish. This is where you cross every *t* and dot every *i*.

Content and structure are still in play, but now you will move from revision to editing and proofreading. By the end of step 10, you should be ready to send in your essay with a completed application to the college of your dreams.

Ready to Write?

Wow's ten steps will help you put your stories on paper in your own words and in your own voice. We don't provide a template, and we never tell anyone what to write. Instead, we teach our students how to draft compelling personal essays. As a result, they end up with beautiful stories and a great sense of pride. What is more, they hear yes from their dream schools, year after year.

Consider our student, Michael, a young man who worked with us on the personal statement for his law school application. At first, he truly believed he could not write. He changed his mind after working closely with a Wow coach. He wrote this to us after he was accepted to law school: "I didn't know I could write. My friends just help each other, and they end up emailing (their essays) back and forth to three or four friends for review. They just keep rewriting without any real input. You taught me a process so I can do this again by myself. You helped me come up with my own ideas."

Here's a comment from a parent in New York whose daughter got into eight schools, including Princeton, Yale, Columbia and Georgetown: "I'm convinced her essays made a big difference, and we are so grateful for everything you did for her."

Finally, we got some kudos from Peter, a transfer student who was already a skillful writer when he came to us: "Wow did much more than help me craft strong and effective essays for my college applications, though they certainly did that too. They taught me to approach writing in a new way, and gave me a process that I will keep with me forever. It is hard to explain just how useful their approach has been, but within minutes of sitting down (and I was skeptical at first), I was in awe of its efficacy."

As we've shown you, we spend a lot of time up front, making sure our students know why they are writing the essay and what they want to say. We make sure that first and foremost, our students understand the prompt and can illustrate something meaningful about themselves. If you put adequate time into preparation, your writing will flow more naturally. Best of all, the essays will turn out better. That's what happens to our students who take the time to get it right at the beginning. Every time. We have never had a student who could not write an effective college essay using our approach.

Once you decide what you want to share with colleges and have chosen an essay topic, you will be ready to start writing. To begin, find a quiet space to write. Just as we tell our students, we'll tell you: Writing is not a group activity. Write your draft. Write it alone.

Our students sometimes ask us which words to use, what types of sentences colleges like, and if there is a way to write to make them sound smarter. The most common question we get comes in the very beginning of the process: Where do I start? We'll tell you what we tell them: Start anywhere. The beginning of the story. The middle. The end. It doesn't matter. Just start.

The essay can be revised later. For the first draft of an essay, you need to get content down on paper. Structure will emerge through the revision process. There's no need to get everything in the ideal order. Don't worry about the opening line. Not in the first draft. At this point, we encourage our students to write too much, then cut and change words and sentences later.

Once the first draft is done, you can ask someone you trust to review the essay for content only. Ask your reviewer to read it without a red pen in hand and without their hands on the computer keyboard. Ask your reader to make sure they know what the essay is about and why you chose this topic. What happened? Why does it matter?

Don't worry about perfection yet, but do ask them to double-check the prompt. If the prompt asks you to reflect on an experience and its influence on you, be sure you have talked about both the experience and its effect.

We respond to first drafts with comments in the form of detailed letters, not marked-up essays. We don't correct grammar and spelling yet because we don't know if those exact words will end up in the final product.

The best way to move the essay along is to ask your reviewer to read with a few questions in mind.

- Is anything missing?
- Is the essay's purpose clear?
- Do I have a solid theme that answers the questions: What happened? Why does it matter?

After the first draft review, your essay will begin to develop through the process of revision. As you revise, try to let go of any preconceived notions about what makes a good essay. It's important to just write. Don't fall in love with your first draft. Be open-minded. Be willing to be surprised.

Many students find that their essays go in wonderful and unexpected directions as they revise. When you understand that revision involves "re-seeing" an essay, it feels less like fixing something that is broken and more like a process of discovery.

Students sometimes try to shortcut the revision process. But when they really take the time to do it right and think like a writer, they are pleased with the results. After one of our students, Sarah, got to college, she sent us a note, saying that learning how to revise made her a better writer and that she "learned to transform something I have written into something totally new. Writing is no longer taking apart something that I made but creating something bigger and better than I had before."

You can have an equally meaningful experience with writing and revision. Once the first draft is complete, our coaches can generally get a student through to the final draft in three additional revisions, but that number is not set in stone. While there is no right or wrong number of drafts, at some point, you will need to let yourself be done. Remember, colleges are not looking for perfection; they are looking for insight into your character.

You'll know you have made it to the final draft once the content is in place, the structure has emerged, the essay clearly responds to the prompt, and the writing flows from beginning to end. That's your cue that it's time to polish. You can now ask someone to check to see if you've crossed every *t* and dotted every *i*.

Share the checklist below with your reader to evaluate a traditional personal statement, such as the Common Application essay, the Coalition for Access, Affordability and Success application, the University of California personal insight questions, ApplyTexas or any primary prompt from schools that use their own applications.

Content Review:

- ☐ Does the essay answer the prompt?
- ☐ Can you tell why I chose this topic?
- ☐ Is the essay about me, or is it really about the place, person or experience featured in the essay?
- ☐ Does it illustrate a trait I want to share with colleges?
- ☐ Does it tell colleges something meaningful about me that is not clear from the rest of my application package?
- ☐ Does the essay sound like me?

Structure Review:

- ☐ Does the first paragraph make you want to keep reading?
- ☐ Does the essay move smoothly from beginning to end?

Polish Review:

- ☐ Does the essay use the same verb tense throughout?
- ☐ Have I avoided sentence fragments and run-on sentences?
- ☐ Is the punctuation correct and consistent?
- ☐ Is every word spelled correctly?

You've made it this far. Give yourself a pat on the back. If you have more questions, let us know. We have more good information, and we're always happy to share.

Trust Yourself

Before we start working with our students, we tell them: "This is your journey, so own the process. When you are done, you will be a more confident, empowered writer, ready for college and your future. Trust yourself!"

We want to share the message with you, too. It does not matter where your story takes place, how large or small it is, or what you did. You matter. Why you did something matters. What you learned matters. How it changed or affected you matters.

Answer the prompt with a story illustrating the trait you want to share in a way that shows how you think, offers insight into your character and helps admissions teams round out your application package. You should trust your own words, style and voice.

Every year, we work with students who tell us they cannot write; they don't believe in themselves. We know better. We challenge them to follow our approach. It works. Every time. Why? With instructions, anyone can learn how to write. Think you can't write? Nonsense.

David was one of those students who lacked the confidence to write his essay. Applying to college was stressful; writing the essays paralyzed him. He came to Wow convinced he just couldn't write.

David had good grades in math and English, and scored well on the ACT (in writing, too). He spoke clearly and articulately. He had good reasons for wanting to study business in college. The boy who said he could not write was a sports reporter for his high school newspaper (and an exceptional varsity hockey player).

Like so many students feeling pressure to get into college, David's fear of writing this essay prevented him from getting the job done.

"Can you think?" we asked him.

"Um, yes," he said.

"Well, then, you can write."

If you can think, you can write. We talked about what mattered to David, and why. Why did he want to go to college? What did he want admissions to know about him? What made him tick? He said everyone thought of him as a gifted hockey player. But he had another side few could see. He was kind and compassionate with a soft spot for special needs children. That, he said, would be a nice thing for colleges to know.

We brainstormed ideas based on what David wanted colleges to know about him. David was afraid to write about hockey. "Everyone" told him not to write about sports. We explained that a college essay was not about an experience; it was about him – his insight into the experience, any experience. If David had a story about sports that demonstrated his kindness and compassion, then it might work.

In the end, David wrote about the moment that his cousin with Down Syndrome, who regularly attended his hockey games, held up a homemade sign to cheer him on during a game. "I just wanted to score one for my cousin," David said.

David's story about his relationship with his disabled cousin turned into an insightful essay, illustrating something meaningful to David that colleges would never have known about him. He used it for two different college applications. It was his genuine story, his idea, and no one else could possibly duplicate it. He was admitted to both schools.

That night, David's mom called. She had never seen her son this excited about anything other than girls or sports. He finally believed he could write.

David listened to his writing voice, and he liked what he heard. You can do the same.

Six

RESOURCES

This section contains the following items:

1. College Essay Do's and Don'ts for Students

2. Tips from Inside the Admissions Office

3. Understanding the Common Application Personal Statement Prompts

4. Testimonials

College Essay Do's and Don'ts for Students

Do

- Follow the instructions, and answer the prompt
- Write about yourself; you are impressive
- Focus on what you learned, and why it matters to you
- Show insight into your character; demonstrate reflection
- Share something meaningful colleges do not already know about you
- Illustrate a positive trait
- Write the essay yourself
- Write it in your own voice, using the words you use every day
- Check spelling and grammar before you click send

Don't

- Write about someone other than yourself
- Focus on your accomplishments or experiences
- Write something that illustrates a negative trait
- Write what you think colleges want to read
- Plagiarize or let anyone write the essay (or a piece of it) for you
- Imitate sample essays you find in books or the Internet
- Believe everything you read: there are no gimmicks, tricks or shortcuts to help you master the essay
- Repeat the question in your answer, or overuse buzzwords (passion, grit, leadership)
- Rely on spell check

Tips from Inside the Admissions Office

Time and again, admissions officers tell us exactly what they want in the essays. Their advice is worth listening to!

Katie Fretwell, Dean of Admission and Financial Aid, Amherst College
"Don't get caught in the 'what do they want to hear?' trap. The essay is about what you want to say. Think about what the rest of your application will already reveal: don't waste the opportunity to let your personality shine by stating the obvious or being redundant in your essay content or message."

Amy Jarich, Associate Vice Chancellor of Admissions & Enrollment (Interim), UC-Berkeley
"I just want to know what you care about. What would you tell me in an elevator? Let me know that you're active and alive in the world you live in."

Shawn Felton, Cornell University, Director of Undergraduate Admissions

"We are creating a class. We look at numbers, grades and test scores. But there's more to it. We are trying to put a face with all this information. We don't care about your passion. There is no passion without core. We care about your convictions. What are your beliefs?"

Christina Lopez, Barnard College, Director of Admissions

"The whole application process is one big 'Match.com' process. The students are creating their profile within their application and reflecting in the essays on who they are as scholars and people."

Tamara Siler, Rice University, Senior Associate Director for Admission

"Students think it has to be a discussion of their most traumatic experiences. If you have a relatively peaceful existence, that is fine."

Jan Deike, Vanderbilt University, Assistant Director of Admissions

"Sometimes students feel that because they haven't found the cure for cancer, they have nothing to share. Life is truly lived in the smaller moments, and that can be a powerful essay."

Jim Cotter, Michigan State University, Director of Admissions

"The essay is value added. At a moderately selective school, it can pull a student on the cusp up. At a highly selective school, a poor statement can make the difference between being admitted or not."

Christoph Guttentag, Duke University, Dean of Undergraduate Admissions

"By the time (the application) comes to us, many of them have gone through so many hands that the essays are sanitized. I wish I saw more of a thoughtful voice of a 17-year-old."

Lorenzo Gamboa, Santa Clara University, Senior Associate Director of Admission

"Students do not need to compile an entire season into an essay. Just give us one place, one time, one moment, and that will do it for you. The key is to show genuine passion, commitment and that they have what it takes to survive at the school."

Calvin Wise, Johns Hopkins University, Director of Recruitment

"I never run into a colleague's office and say, 'look at this 4.0 GPA.' I will run into an office with a good essay to share; that excites me."

Kim Bryant, University of Michigan, Assistant Director of Admissions

"This is your interview. Let me know who you really are."

Understanding the Common Application Personal Statement Prompts

Every few years, the Common Application, a tool used by more than 700 colleges to help students apply seamlessly to multiple schools, makes noticeable changes to its essay prompts. The changes are based on feedback from students, parents, high school counselors, educational consultants and member schools following each admissions cycle.

In 2017, the Common App added two new prompts for the next group of college applicants; they also tweaked some of the existing questions. The revisions to prompts 2, 3 and 5 clarified the purpose of those questions, while the new prompts provide a few more options.

Reflection Matters Most

The changes reinforce the message we share with our students: At its core, a personal statement is all about reflection. An effective essay shows insight into a college applicant's character because it answers two central questions: 1) What happened? and 2) Why does it matter?

Why a topic matters to a student (the reflection) is more important than what happened (the experience, the activity, the idea, the concept, or the person who influenced that student).

Just to confirm that we understood the purpose of the changes, we went straight to the source – Scott Anderson, Senior Director of Education and Partnerships for the Common Application. He said:

> "The prompts have changed slightly, but the instructions remain the same: What do you want application readers to know about you? The prompts simply serve to help students approach that question from as many angles as possible, whether it be maturity, identity, curiosity, pastimes, aspirations, community, relationships, or anything else. Students should pick the prompt that supports and gets them excited about the story they want to tell about themselves."

Here's our take on the seven options, straight from Wow Online – College Essay. We spend a lot of time with our private coaching students making sure they understand the prompts before they dive in and draft an essay. It saves them a lot of time on unnecessary drafts that miss the mark.

Prompt 1

Some students have a background, identity, interest, or talent that is so meaningful they believe their application would be incomplete without it. If this sounds like you, then please share your story.

The key word in this prompt is "meaningful."

Ultimately, your essay is not about your background, identity, interest, talent or experience; it's about you. What did you learn about yourself? What made it meaningful? Admissions officers read these essays to find out something they don't already know about you. They can tell from your application that you are on the lacrosse team or in the school orchestra. They know you worked as a researcher or a hospital aide or a bagger in a grocery store. And if your transcript says you took American Literature, they can assume you read books like *A Raisin in the Sun*, *The Crucible* or *The Bluest Eye*.

They don't know how those experiences affected you, whom you met along the way or why a piece of music is so important to you. They have no idea how you have changed and why you might be a good fit for their school. You can share these insights in your essay.

You could respond to this prompt by sharing any type of story – a description of a meaningful conversation, a moment when you realized something important about yourself – anything that truly and vividly demonstrates who you are. Your experience does not have to be particularly impressive; you do not have to share a story about climbing a mountain or rescuing three children from a burning building. You could write about babysitting or making meatballs with your grandmother, navigating an icy highway or playing basketball with friends. Your challenge is to find a story that illustrates something meaningful. Choose a moment, then explore it in detail.

Prompt 2

The lessons we take from obstacles we encounter can be fundamental to later success. Recount a time when you faced a challenge, setback, or failure. How did it affect you, and what did you learn from the experience?

Prompt #2 is more specific than #1. The key sentence is at the end of this prompt. Your readers are not going to judge you because you failed at something. Everyone faces obstacles. They are asking you to reflect on the experience, to demonstrate how you grew or changed as a result.

What do you want readers to know about you? Do you have a story about facing a challenge, setback or failure that shows you are resilient, or demonstrates that you learned to be a leader? If you do, this may be a good prompt for you.

Prompt 3
Reflect on a time when you questioned or challenged a belief or idea. What prompted your thinking? What was the outcome?

Prompt #3 also asks for reflection. During high school, you are constantly asked to look toward the future: Where are you going? What do you want to do with your life? Where will you attend college? What career will you pursue? Your college application essay offers an opportunity to look back, and this prompt is a prime example.

In this case, the central story should showcase a time when you challenged a belief or idea. Maybe the idea was religious or political. Perhaps it was a family rule or a school requirement. Did you challenge something you had always believed in, or question something you had long felt uncomfortable with?

Prompt 4
Describe a problem you've solved or a problem you'd like to solve. It can be an intellectual challenge, a research query, an ethical dilemma – anything that is of personal importance, no matter the scale. Explain its significance to you and what steps you took or could be taken to identify a solution.

Prompt #4 invites you to share something about yourself through a challenge you've experienced.

The key phrases here are "of personal importance" and "explain its significance." By asking about a problem you care about and how you solved (or would solve) it, readers hope to learn something about you, about how you think and problem-solve.

Whether you choose a problem you've solved or a problem you would like to resolve, college admissions officers want to read a meaningful story about your experience dealing with a challenge, be it intellectual, ethical or academic in nature. The topic is secondary; the subject is YOU! What did you learn? Why was it significant?

You might describe the time you got locked out of a house one night when you were babysitting. But remember, that description is meaningless unless you focus on why the experience was meaningful to you. To do this, show some reflection. If you figured out a way to turn the challenge into a fun adventure for the kids, and they never felt scared, describe what it meant to you. Why did it matter? Draw the reader in.

Prompt 5

Discuss an accomplishment, event, or realization that sparked a period of personal growth and a new understanding of yourself or others.

Prompt #5 is more specific, but still leaves room for reflection and interpretation.

Note that this prompt asks you to discuss something you accomplished, an experience or something you realized that sparked growth and understanding. You do not have to show that you mastered something challenging. In this case, you are being asked to demonstrate how you have grown in your understanding. What do you know or understand now that you didn't know before?

Prompt 6

Describe a topic, idea, or concept you find so engaging that it makes you lose all track of time. Why does it captivate you? What or who do you turn to when you want to learn more?

The key word in prompt #6 is "engaging," but you don't have to impress with big ideas. Try asking yourself questions like these: Why is this topic, idea or concept so engaging? How does it make me feel? Who do I talk to about these ideas? Where do I go to research new concepts?

Maybe you care about social justice. Perhaps you're captivated by humor or technology. You can explore the concept overall or share an example of that concept in action. Whether you collected clothes and toiletries for a local family who lost their home in a fire or attracted ten thousand followers by tweeting a daily joke, why did you do it? How does that activity demonstrate how you think, problem-solve or process information?

Prompt 7

Share an essay on any topic of your choice. It can be one you've already written, one that responds to a different prompt, or one of your own design.

The key word is "choice." And while this prompt appears to be different from the others, the purpose is the same. Yes, applicants can submit any essay they want, but as the overall instructions clearly state, even an A+ paper must still illustrate something meaningful about you.

Suppose you want to submit a critical analysis you wrote for Honors English about a character in *Jane Eyre*. Could it work? Maybe. Ask yourself what the essay demonstrates about you. Do you yearn for more than what traditional society allows, like Jane? Does the paper demonstrate how the book propelled you toward political activism? Does it show how the book changed you? After admissions officers read the paper, will they learn something new about you? If not, it won't work as a college essay, no matter how well-written.

Testimonials

Laura, parent, Scottsdale, AZ
"Wow was a phenomenal resource in teaching both of my twin boys how to write their college entrance essays! The process was smooth, and I was incredibly impressed when I read their final drafts. Wow helped each boy's own voice and ideas come through."

Sydney, student, Novi, MI
"I like that Wow is an outside source and can make unbiased suggestions. Wow lets you do the work so your essay is in your voice, and they're also very quick at getting back to you. Writing papers and essays has never been something that I enjoy but, after working with Wow, I learned some techniques to improve my writing. Wow gave me the confidence to use my own style rather than a formal style with fancy words."

Emma, student, Washington, D.C.
"I liked working with Wow Writing Workshop because I felt like I was in charge of my essay. The final product of my essay sounded just like me. It's a really personal story and you can tell a lot about who I am from the story and my voice."

Jonathon, parent, Brooklyn, NY
"You gave us a true Wow evaluation. My son felt his essays were stronger, and I certainly thought they were much better, after your editorial input."

Jen, high school counselor, Monroe, MI
"We read a lot of essays, and we know what sounds good, but we are not writing teachers. We used Wow's tips for writing college essays this year with all of our seniors, and the information was so valuable their essays were the best ever."

Anita, parent, Denver, CO
"You are magicians! My daughter was so excited after starting her essay. She is in her room writing away. I can't believe this is my child."

David, student, New York City
"Your assistance has done wonders for me. Thanks again for all you have done, as you have a true talent for coaching and editing."

Bruce, parent, Brooklyn, NY
"I really appreciated that my son and I had Wow as a sounding board throughout the essay writing process. His essays were more personal and engaging after working with Wow. He really enjoyed the experience, and benefited from your comments and attention."

Grant, student, Palo Alto, CA
"I liked how each step in the Wow Method built on the last so that the essay continued to grow and improve. Instructions were clear and provided specific details on how to problem solve and revise, which was helpful."

Spencer, student, Franklin, MI

"Wow helped me expand my ideas and shape them into great college essays. I had never been told before that I am a good writer. Their confidence in me changed the way that I think about writing and I am definitely a better writer for it."

Be Social

If you liked *How to Write an Effective College Application Essay*, please help other parents find this book.

1. Write a review on Amazon.com; share it on your own social media channels.

2. Sign up for Wow's free tip sheet and other resources for students. https://wowwritingworkshop.com/college-essay-writing/students/.

3. Like Wow's Facebook page. www.facebook.com/wowwriting/.

4. Follow Wow on Twitter. https://twitter.com/wowwriting.

5. Watch our video interviews with admissions officers on YouTube. https://www.youtube.com/user/wowwritingworkshop.

For information about Wow's private coaching & essay review services, or the College Essay Crash Course, visit our website: WowWritingWorkshop.com.

About the Authors

Kim Lifton, President of Wow Writing Workshop, can get a story out of anyone. Perceptive, resourceful and curious, she keeps her finger on the pulse of the college admissions industry. She also works with Wow's corporate and nonprofit clients. A former journalist, Kim speaks at schools and industry conferences throughout the U.S.; her articles on the college essay appear regularly in print and on the web. Kim's work has been featured in a variety of newspapers, magazines and online publications.

Susan Knoppow, CEO of Wow Writing Workshop, can turn the most daunting writing challenge into a series of simple steps. Focused, incisive and creative, Susan developed the Wow Method for teaching writing. A dynamic presenter, Susan also trains counselors, consultants and educators to guide their students through the essay-writing process. A former executive speechwriter and copywriter, she also works with Wow's corporate and nonprofit clients, and speaks at schools and industry events. She is a published poet and essayist.

Made in the USA
Coppell, TX
08 February 2021

49974290R00066